COLO

EXTERIORS

THE SANCTUARY

THE PORTICO DE LA GLORIA

THE RADIATING CHAPELS

THE CHAPELS ON THE NORTH SIDE-AISLE

THE MUSEUMS

THE CROSSING

RS

- **I** THE OBRADOIRO FAÇADE
- **II** PLATERIAS
- **III** THE CLOCK TOWER
- **IV** QUINTANA AND THE PUERTA SANTA
- **V** THE AZABACHERIA FAÇADE

THE INTERIOR

- **1** THE SANCTUARY
- **2** THE APOSTLE'S CHAMBER
- **3** THE BURIAL CRYPT
- **4** THE PORTICO DE LA GLORIA
- **5** THE OUR LADY OF THE PILLAR CHAPEL
- **6** THE MONDRAGON CHAPEL
- **7** THE AZUCENA CHAPEL
- **8** THE PUERTA SANTA
- **9** THE SAVIOUR CHAPEL
- **10** THE OUR LADY OF THE SNOWS CHAPEL
- **11** THE ST. JOHN THE APOSTLE CHAPEL
- **12** THE CHAPEL OF THE IMMACULATE CONCEPTION
- **13** THE HOLY SPIRIT CHAPEL
- **14** THE CHURCH OF LA CORTICELA
- **15** ST. ANDREW'S CHAPEL
- **16** ST. ANTHONY'S CHAPEL
- **17** ST. CATHERINE'S CHAPEL
- **18** THE COMMUNION CHAPEL
- **19** THE CHRIST OF BURGOS CHAPEL

THE MUSEUMS

- **20** THE RELICS CHAPEL
- **21** ST. FERDINAND'S CHAPEL
- **22** THE SACRISTY
- **23** THE CLOISTERS
- **24** THE DAWN CHAPEL
- **25** THE CHAPTER ARCHIVES
- **26** THE CHAPTER LIBRARY
- **27** THE CHAPTER HOUSE
- **28** THE TAPESTRY MUSEUM
- **29** THE ARCHAEOLOGICAL MUSEUM
- **30** THE CRYPT BENEATH THE PORTICO

VISITOR'S GUIDE

THE CATHEDRAL OF SANTIAGO DE COMPOSTELA

Jesús Precedo Lafuente

Palacios y MUSEOS

Legal Deposit: M-36042-1998

I.S.B.N.: 84-8003-108-5

Design: Juan M. Domínguez and Rosa Mayer

Layout: Myriam López Consalvi

Coordination: ALDEASA

Text: Jesús Precedo Lafuente

Translation: Nigel Williams

Photographs: Manuel González Vicente

Photomechanical Production: Lucam

Printed in Spain by: Estudios Gráficos Europeos. S.A.

CONTENTS

View of the Cathedral from Paseo de la Herradura.

The Casa del Cabildo *or Town Hall in Plaza de Platerías.*

Detail from the fountain in Plaza de Platerías.

INTRODUCTION

THE FOUR *PLAZAS*

Four *Plazas* surround the Cathedral of Santiago de Compostela. Two bear the names of crafts: to the south **Plateros** ("Silversmiths") and to the north **Azabacheros** ("Jetworkers"), where the original name of the ancient Romanesque façade – El Paraíso ("Paradise") – was changed in the last century to La Inmaculada in homage to the mystery of the Immaculate Conception, defined as a dogma of

(Left) Plaza de Platerías and (right) Plaza de la Quintana.

A tour of the façades
Before entering the Cathedral it is particularly important to walk around the building in order to view its four façades and, above all, to discover what remains of the beauty of its original Romanesque construction.

Christian faith by Pope Pius IX. The west square was named after the stonecutter's workshop in which, with hammer and pick, various generations of workmen interpreted the mysterious language of stone; and, to the east, stand the **Quintana de Muertos** and **Quintana de Vivos**.

Once a cemetery, the **Plaza de los Muertos** ("Square of the Dead") is now completely paved over and stretches from the Cathedral to the Benedictine Monastery of San Paio de Antealtares.

THE THIRD CATHEDRAL

Work on the Romanesque cathedral began in 1075. With time, however, features of successive architectural styles were added in evidence of the subsequent rectors' acceptance of the tastes of their age. On some occasions the new additions were completely different in style from the original Romanesque features, while on others only modifications were made – as in the case of the Azabachería and Obradoiro façades.

This, Santiago's third known Cathedral, was built in the times of Bishop Diego Peláez and Alfonso VI. Of the two earlier "known" cathedrals (for it cannot be said that there have not been others) perfectly identifiable vestiges associated with Alfonso II and Alfonso III have survived. The remains of these two churches – in no way comparable with the Cathedral as it is today – lie next to a necropolis and close to the old city walls and defence tower under the Basilica's floor. What is left of this cemetery, which served the town throughout the first eight centuries of the Christian era, provides magnificent evidence (far fewer records exist from that period than from later times) of the settlement of what is now known as Compostela.

The Hostal de los Reyes Católicos, *the* Palacio de Gelmírez *and the Cathedral in Plaza del Obradoiro.*

Statue of St James above the Puerta Santa.

THE NAME "COMPOSTELA"

The name of the town has not always been **Santiago de Compostela**, for originally it was the "Lugar Santo" or "Holy Place" in reference to remains venerated there and was also known as "Arca Marmórica" ("Ark of Marble").

Only later did the name Santiago (from the name of the apostle St James in Spanish) de Compostela come to be used. It has often been said that Compostela means "Campo de la Estrella" ("Field of the Star"), but this would appear to be no more than an ingenious, rather facile invention. "Compostela", however, seems to imply a piece of land or a well-tended tomb – certainly no less appropriate an explanation.

Still associated with the streets of Compostela, **Campo de la Estrella** would seem to refer to the celestial light which appeared to the hermit Pelayo in the 9th century and came to rest over a certain place. Pelayo interpreted the light as a sign from God and began to dig, subsequently reporting the great event to Alfonso II and Bishop Theodomir. Theodomir, who was Bishop of Iria Flavia, 17 kilometres from Compostela, was so moved that he gave orders that when he died he was to be buried in the town. His tombstone can still be seen inside the cathedral.

The Cathedral roof with the Obradoiro façade seen from the rear. (Facing page) a view of the Obradoiro façade.

EXTERIORS

I THE OBRADOIRO FAÇADE

Although the tour of the Cathedral could begin at any point, for practical purposes it is advisable to walk around the outside first. The **Obradoiro façade** was built in the 18th century, replacing a Romanesque front whose features cannot now be seen due to the changes made to the porch known as the Pórtico de la Gloria, which faces west; this great work of art by master Fernando de Casas y Nóvoa was erected in the wake of the damage done by the ravages of time to the original polychrome and due to a new taste for Baroque exuberance. A large number of artists collaborated with Casas y Nóvoa, including the sculptors and woodcarvers Gregorio Fernández, Antonio Vaamonde, Lens, Gambino, Nogueira, Pose, López, Ramos and Montero and the painter García Bouzas. The Baroque towers of La Carraca on the north side and Las Campanas (on which master Peña de Toro collaborated) on the south were raised on top of the Romanesque ones. Particularly important in the iconography on the Pórtico de la Gloria are the figures of St. James and his two disciples, Anastasius and Theodore. Next to these are

Scallop in the Platerías façade.

The Creation of Adam *in the Platerías façade.*

the figures of SS. James the Less, Barbara, John the Evangelist and also Susanna.

Two stairways, both dating from the 17th century, lead up from the square to the Cathedral. Beneath these is a church wrongly known as the **Old Cathedral**, built to fill the available space at a time when bringing in building materials was a costly affair. Three other buildings stand on the square. Opposite the Obradoiro façade is the **palace** named after Archbishop **Rajoy**, who ordered it built as a *Consistorio* (Town Hall) and residence for the Cathedral confessors. It currently houses the offices of the City Council and the President of the Galician Regional Government or *Xunta.* To the right, the **Colegio de San Jerónimo de Artistas** dates from the 17th century, although the 15th-century frontispiece belonged to another building which previously stood on the site. The **Hospital Real**, on the left, was founded by the Catholic Monarchs for pilgrims and now serves as a hotel.

II PLATERIAS

The **Platerías façade** is the only one to have retained its Romanesque structure despite a number of modifications and the addition of figures from other parts of the Cathedral – all of which makes it difficult to analyze. It would seem, however, to

depict "Christ the Light of the World". Certain mythological features added to it (possibly soon after it was built) have subsequently been reinterpreted on a Christian basis. The main figure is Christ the King accompanied by saints and with Abraham, admiring his descendant, at his feet. Due to its horns the figure at the bottom may be that of Moses in a reference to the light with which his face shone after his meeting with God. The scene also contains the figures of five apostles, two of which are damaged and cannot be identified; the other three are St John, St Peter and St James. A Latin inscription on James's halo identifies him: *Iacobus Zebedei*. He is flanked by the trunks of two trees which may be cypresses. To his right, the monarch on whose orders the present Cathedral was built is also identified in an inscription:

The Platerías façade, David (left) and Christ in Majesty (right).

The figures on the Platerías façade

Despite the ravages of time, these sculptures are still highly impressive. We find before us a mixture of archaism and an abundance of perfect forms. The main theme on the tympana is the humbleness of the incarnation while on the section of wall around the upper area it is the glory of exaltation.

(Above) the façade and the Fuente de los Caballos *in Plaza de Platerías.*

(Right) tympanum in the Platerías façade.

(Facing page) the Rúa do Villar *with the Clock Tower in the background.*

davina

The clock face in the tower of the same name. Curiously it has an hour hand only.

Alfonso Rey. Particularly worthy of mention on the left-hand side of the entrance is a statue of David playing the rebec. The tympanum on the left displays the Temptations of Christ, while that on the right is divided into two parts, the upper depicting the Adoration of the Magi and the lower scenes from the Passion. The original work on this façade is attributed to masters Bernardo and Roberto.

III THE CLOCK TOWER

The Plateresque construction on the left was designed by Rodrigo Gil de Hontañón and dates from the 16th century. The echeloned **tower** at the south end is known as the **Torre**

del Tesoro ("Tower of the Treasure") as it holds ornaments and other objects related to worship. It seems that its shape, reminiscent of Chinese architecture, is due to influence from the Americas. Some writers, however, consider that this kind of tower is a homage to Divine Motherhood. Another tower, which stands closer to the Fonseca building, is known as the Torre de la Vela.

To the right, the **Clock Tower** is a mixture of Gothic and Baroque. The first section, which is cube-shaped, is Gothic and was built in the 14th century on the orders of Archbishop Rodrigo del Padrón. Its name – La Berenguela – may be due to the fact that it was fortified by Archbishop Berenguel de Landoira in order to defend himself from the attacks of the Compostela bourgeoisie. Another theory, however, is that, being slender, it

(Top left) the wall of the Benedictine Monastery of San Pelayo de Antealtares, (bottom left) Plaza de la Quintana, and (right) the Puerta Real *or* Puerta Quintana.

The "Puerta Real"
Also known as the "Quintana Door" this is the most majestic of the three doors in the east façade. On All Souls' Day – 2nd November – the Chapter comes to the door in procession to pray for the dead buried in La Quintana. Built between 1658 and 1661, its inner face is thought to be Compostela's first Baroque work.

The "Puerta Santa"
The "Holy Door" is opened on the evening of 31st December before a Holy Year in accordance with an ancient rite. The celebration of the Holy Year in Compostela has taken place since the 12th century whenever the Apostle's feast day – 25th July – has fallen on a Sunday. This takes place in a sequence of 6, 5, 6, 11 years. The last Holy Year in this century will be 1999.

(Above) the façade with the Puerta Santa *in Plaza de la Quintana. (Facing page) the Azabachería façade.*

was named after Queen Berenguela. The Baroque section was built by Domingo Antonio de Andrade in the 17th century. The present clock mechanism was made in Ferrol in the 19th century by Antelo. The clock faces display the hour hands only and two recently restored bells chime the quarter-hour and the hour.

IV QUINTANA AND THE PUERTA SANTA

The area in front of the Cathedral's east end is called **La Quintana**, which means Plaza or Square. The upper part is known as "Los Vivos" ("The Quick") and the larger, lower area as "Los Muertos" ("The Dead"). For a long time it was a cemetery. The

Panels with apostles and prophets flanking the Puerta Santa. *(Facing page) view of the high altar.*

large section of wall directly opposite the Cathedral forms part of the Benedictine Convent of St. Pelayo de Antealtares, previously a monastery closely linked to the cult of St. James in which the Benedictine monks alternated with the Cathedral canons. Nine sections, some circular and others polygonal, were added to the Cathedral's large apse. However, as time passed yet more new constructions were built, some for worship, others for defence and offices, all of which upset the original structural harmony, so that in the 17th century the Cathedral Chapter decided to remodel the area through a project designed by Vega y Verdugo and implemented by José de la Peña. Of the doors on this side the most striking is the Real ("Royal") on the far left.

The **Puerta Santa** ("Holy Door") is opened on the 31st December before a "Holy" or "Jubilee" year in Compostela. A small, Romanesque door inside is one of the nine with which the Cathedral was originally endowed. The façade dates from the 17th century. The twenty-four small statues adorning it depict apostles and prophets and came from the stone choir carved by master Mateo. The three larger statues of the Pilgrim Apostle and his two disciples Anastasius and Theodore above the façade were carved by Pedro Docampo in 1694.

V THE AZABACHERIA FAÇADE

To the left of the Quintana stairs is the Parish Church of La Corticela, built as an oratory possibly in the 9th century. It was attended by the monks of San Paio even after they had built the Monastery of San Martín Pinario. It is now a parish church for foreign pilgrims and is also dedicated to more secular purposes.

The **Azabachería façade** takes its name from the jetworkers' guild, to which the street leading into the Cathedral's north square was dedicated. According to the *Codex Calixtinus* its old name was "Paraíso" ("Paradise") deriving from the stories told by its Romanesque sculptures. Here the French route to Santiago ended. The first manifestation of Compostela Neo-Classicism, this façade was built by Ventura Rodríguez, Luca Ferro Caaveiro and Clemente Fernández Sarela among others. Ferro and Fernández began the work but due to certain discrepancies Domingo Lois Monteagudo, who had studied under Ventura Rodríguez, was commissioned to continue it, although he may actually have only made changes to the iconography. The statue of Faith was carved by Gambino and those of St James the Pilgrim, Alfonso III and Ordoño II and the portraits of Charles III and his wife Maria Amalia of Saxony by Máximo Salazar.

(Left) one of the pulpits and (right) the image of St James on the high altar.

The pulpits
Similar in design, both pulpits were made by Juan Bautista Celma, who produced a large number of sculptures and paintings for the Cathedral. Celma placed his signature on them in 1583, also stating that he was Aragonese. The sounding-boards were made by Miguel Romay in 1714.

THE INTERIOR

I THE SANCTUARY

Once inside the Cathedral, the first visit made should be to the **high altar**, above the Apostle's tomb. Constructed in the Baroque style under the supervision of Canon Vega y Verdugo, it erased all traces of the Romanesque work, which had already been modified in the 15th and 16th centuries. As it was necessary to adapt the ciborium or canopy (by Domingo Antonio de Andrade) to the available space, it is out of proportion, though nevertheless of great beauty. Among the artists who worked on the **sanctuary** were: the masters Francisco de Antas and Bernardo Cabrera; the Flemish marble workers Gutier, Sameria and Broces;

(Left) a detail from the Choir and (right) an alms box with the image of St Salome.

the sculptors Pedro del Valle and Mateo de Prado; and various Compostela woodcarvers.

The sanctuary contains three images of St James. The one at the bottom, from Mateo's workshop, is of St James the Teacher; the next is of St James the Pilgrim; and the third is of St James the Knight (by Mateo de Prado). Paying homage to St James are four Spanish kings closely associated with devotion to the saint: Alfonso II, Ramiro I, Ferdinand V and Philip IV. At the four corners are statues representing the Cardinal Virtues: Prudence, Justice, Fortitude and Temperance.

The **choir stalls** were made when the old choir at the centre of the Cathedral was removed. They were designed by Martínez Pidal and Pons Sorolla and built by Del Río in 1949. Of the lamps, three are of special interest: the one on the right was

The alms boxes

Two alms boxes are attached to the pulpits. The one on the right dates from 1527 and stands at the foot of a stone image of St Salome, who was St James's mother and a relative of the Virgin Mary's. The one on the left dates from 1497 and displays an image of St James the Less, son of Alphaeus.

St James the Apostle's tomb with figures of the Saviour and the apostles.

donated by María I; that on the left by Archbishop Monroy; and that in the centre by Canon Diego Juan de Ulloa.

The **high altar** was remade by Constenla in 1879. The silver was donated by Archbishop Antonio de Monroy (who was born in Querétaro, Mexico) and sent to Spain from his homeland. With this silver Antonio de Montaos made the frontal and the steps, and Juan de Figueroa the tabernacle and the display cabinet. The image of the Immaculate Conception, designed by Manuel de Prado, was carved by the sculptor Francisco Pecul.

The two **pulpits** were made by the Aragonese Juan Bautista de Celma. The one on the left reproduces scenes from Antonio de Arfe's monstrance, while that on the right displays scenes on the theme of St James as the protector of all of Spain.

The image of St James the Apostle

There are three depictions of St James: in the chamber, he sits as a Teacher receiving pilgrims at his tomb; above it he is depicted as St James the Missionary, preacher of the faith; and on the baldachin he is St James the Warrior, defender of the Christians during the Reconquest and at other times of war.

II THE APOSTLE'S CHAMBER

The pilgrim may approach the polychrome stone seated image of St James the Teacher, made by the school of master Mateo, to embrace it. Archbishop Monroy donated the cape and the staff, both made by Figueroa. Without doubt the custom of embracing the Apostle had much to do with the pilgrim's joy, when, having fulfilled his obligations (among these confessing his sins), he came like the prodigal son in the gospel to be reconciled with the father of all Spaniards in the faith. It is said that before the halo was added to the statue, pilgrims placed their hats on the Apostle's head to embrace him more easily. Above the pilgrim's head is the votive lamp made from the silver hilts of weapons donated by Fernández de Córdoba, the "Great Captain", in 1512, when he came to Compostela as a pilgrim.

Detail from St James's tomb.

III THE BURIAL CRYPT

The **tomb of St James** and his two disciples **Anastasius and Theodore** should be visited next. It has often been asked how the body of an apostle of Christ came to rest in such a remote place as Finisterre. According to tradition St James actually preached in these parts. If this is so and such testimonies were previous to the rediscovery of the tomb in the 9th century (after a period of relative oblivion), it is not difficult to accept that the Apostle was indeed buried in Compostela. The crypt is situated at the end of a cemetery – in use between the 1st and the 8th century – facing the Quintana de Muertos. After the period of relative neglect that ended in the 9th century during the time of Bishop Theodomir and Alfonso II, the Apostle's remains were not hidden again until the period between the time of the Englishman Drake's incursion in the 16th century and 29th January 1879. The successive alterations made to this area now make it impossible to know exactly how it was in antiquity, but enough remains exist to give a general idea. It was indeed a Roman construction dating from the 1st and 2nd centuries and of a type that has been unearthed elsewhere. It had two chambers: a lower one – the tomb itself – and an upper one which served as an oratory and a meeting place. Historically, it is important to bear in mind the subsequent structures, the Muslim invasion and the alterations made to the site, particularly in the 12th and 17th centuries.

Stairs at the tomb.

Work on the crypt as it is today began in 1879, continuing along the lines taken by the historian and Cathedral Canon López Ferreiro. Every effort was made to evoke the old adornment. In July 1884 the

Mass before the tomb.

(Left) the vault above the Pórtico de la Gloria *and (right) the boss in its upper section. (Overleaf) the nave and the Baroque organs.*

The organs
The two organs in the centre of the nave were made by Manuel de la Viña. They are supported by columns from the 17th-century choir. The Baroque adornment was made by Miguel Romay between 1705 and 1712. When the Choir stood at the centre of the nave it formed, together with the organs and the sanctuary, a continuous display of 17th-century art.

silver casket containing the three bodies, (recomposed and classified at that time by professors from the Santiago de Compostela Faculty of Medicine) each in a different compartment, was placed in position. It occupies the site of the original burial, although in a higher position, as the current crypt lies at the same level as the upper section of the Roman construction. Designed by Losada, the casket was made by the local silversmiths Rey and Martínez in imitation of the altarpiece (dating from the time of Archbishop Gelmírez) which stood behind the altar in the 12th century. The lid displays the Christogram – the symbol of the Greek name of Christ in the form of an X and a P which correspond to J and R. Depicted on the front and sides are the Saviour, flanked by ovals, with the apostles beneath arches. The rock crystal cross on the altar was donated by Archbishop Gaspar de Zúñiga y Avellaneda in 1569.

The dome.

(Facing page) view of the Pórtico de la Gloria.

IV THE PÓRTICO DE LA GLORIA

Towards the Pórtico

The Pórtico de la Gloria can now be reached by walking down the aisle. Together with the westernmost structure, which was lost when the Obradoiro façade was built, it was exposed to the elements, with the consequent deterioration of the painting and even the stonework. On the way to the Pórtico de la Gloria, the lamps and organs may be admired. However, to see the Gothic **dome**, which rises to a height of 32 metres and was finished in 1445, it is necessary to look up. The corners display the arms of Archbishop Lope de Mendoza, during whose pontificate the dome was completed. The balcony around the inner face dates from the 17th century and José de la Peña de Toro was commissioned with

(Top left) detail from the base of the Pórtico de la Gloria. *(Top right) Christ in Majesty. (Bottom) detail from a column in the* Pórtico de la Gloria.

the ornamentation. Made in Vizcaya in 1602, the system of pulleys used for the *botafumeiro* or incense burner (discussed later) was devised by Juan Bautista de Celma.

The first lamp on the way to the Pórtico de la Gloria came from the Senate and was donated by Montero Ríos, a local resident. This is followed by two **organs**, both dating from the 18th century, which can be played from the same console. The cases were made by Manuel de la Viña between 1704 and 1712. The **lamp** was displayed at the Paris International Exhibition of 1855. Its decorative elements include acanthus leaves, branches, filaments and rock crystal. Donated by Canon Pedro Méndez Acuña, it was offered to the Cathedral in his name by relatives.

Information on the Pórtico de la Gloria

It is said that when Ferdinand II visited Compostela in the 12th century, the west side of the cathedral was either unfinished or in poor condition, and that the king decided to leave his palace architect, Mateo, behind in Santiago with sufficient funds to finish the work. This took place at the time when the so-called "Beati" codices were being copied from the manuscript of Beatus of Liébana, who in the 8th century had made commentaries on the Book of Revelation, all of which brought this last book of the Holy Scriptures into vogue and prompted the appearance of the famous miniatures of the new school led by Magius. Indeed

(Left) detail from the prophets and (right) the prophet Daniel.

the Pórtico de la Gloria clearly displays the influence of the Book of Revelation.

As it was not common practice to keep a record of the architectural work carried out on the Cathedral, there is no official description of the Pórtico de la Gloria. It is therefore possible only to speculate on the meaning conveyed by this "book" written in the polychrome stone which, like sculptures and paintings in any church, was intended to enlighten the faithful on the mysteries of the faith. The most probable hypothesis is that the Pórtico de la Gloria depicts two of the most important aspects of the Church: the Militant and Triumphant.

Virtually nothing is known about **Mateo**, although there are theories on certain homonymous contemporaries of his who may have been either the master himself or some relative. Some accounts refer to him as a Galician but others, referring to certain influences evident in his art, say that he came from beyond the Pyrenees. There is no doubt, however, as to his skill, which is so wonderfully reflected in this work. Is the orant statue facing the altar a self-portrait? It may well be. The posture reflects piety, humility and thankfulness to God. In any case it is known as the *Santo dos Croques.*

Christ, the Apostles and the Prophets

St Paul wrote on redemption in his epistle to the Ephesians: "Ye are fellow-citizens with the saints, and of the household of God; and are built upon the foundation of the apostles and prophets". In his

The Pórtico de la Gloria
The Pórtico de la Gloria is considered one of the most outstanding examples of mediaeval art. An inscription on the lintels of the central arch of this major work reads: "In the year of the Incarnation of the Lord, 1188, in the era 1226, and on the first day of April, the lintels of the main porch of the Church of Blessed St James were placed in position by master Mateo, who directed the work [on the Cathedral] from [the time of the laying of] its foundations".
The Cathedral possesses the document in which Ferdinand II granted master Mateo, "One hundred *morabetinos*" of gold per year "for all the time of his life so that the work on the Cathedral may be attended to with zeal".

(Left) the angel with the trumpet announcing the Last Judgement referred to in the gospel according to St Matthew. (Right) four of the apostles: Peter, Paul, James and John the Evangelist.

The figures of the apostles
Another great innovation on the Pórtico de la Gloria can be seen in the apostles, who, like the Prophets, are all perfectly represented and seem to be holding a conversation or relating in one way or another with each other.

work, it is quite clear that Mateo bore the doctrine contained in these words carefully in mind. The principal figure (almost three metres high) on the Pórtico de la Gloria is of Christ, seated and revealing the glorious wounds in his hands.

He is accompanied by the four evangelists, two on each side, their symbols making identification easy: St Mark with the lion, St Luke with the ox and St John with the eagle, although St Matthew appears without the angel. On the lower part of the arch, angels carry instruments associated with the Passion, while above are twenty-four musicians (the elders mentioned in the Revelation) with musical instruments. Particularly interesting is the *organistrum* with its strings and sounding wheel. The small images beneath these (miniatures being used to depict a multitude) represent the faithful who have already gone to heaven.

The figures on the right are apostles; beginning from the inside, they are Peter, Paul, James and his brother, John the Evangelist, while those on the left are Prophets, representing, in the same order as the apostles, Moses, Isaiah, Daniel and Jeremiah. The monstrous creatures on the bases are reminiscent of the hybrid guardians found in Assyrian and Babylonian palaces and may represent the vices crushed by the Church. The figure at the centre who is prising open the mouths of two lions with his hands may represent the Celestial Father, Creator of the Universe.

Jews and Gentiles

In the Bible, mankind is divided up into two groups: Jews – members of the people of Israel, into whose number Christ was born – and gentiles.

(Left) St James the Apostle on the trumeau and (right) musicians.

The musician-elders

The archivolt above the tympanum is adorned with twenty-four seated figures holding musical instruments. They represent the twenty-four elders described in the Revelation of St John; "And round about the throne... I saw four and twenty elders sitting, clothed in white raiment; and they had on their heads crowns of gold." (Rev. 4:4).

Column of Jesse or of the Trinity.

Here also are the two divisions of mankind called to form part of the Church. On the right, between the central and side arches, are naked figures, one of which an angel covers with a cloak in a symbol of baptism and grace. On the left, also naked, are the representatives of the Jews, bearing a cartouche recalling the books of the Old Testament – the Jewish Scriptures.

The arch on the right displays strange animals gripping men in their claws. Without any doubt these represent the vices which enslave mankind. On the arch on the left are three archivolts adorned with foliage and a number of human figures. These represent mankind awaiting the coming of the Messiah. On the lower archivolt, Adam and Eve see God's Messenger, who has come to free the universe from their sin.

The Christological Column

In the middle of the central arch and beneath the seated figure of St. James the Great (who holds a tau-staff and a cartouche with the inscription "the Lord sent me") is a white porphyry column which offers a lesson in Christology, for here artistic representations of the human and divine origin of Christ come together. The human aspect is seen on the shaft in the form of a tree sprouting from the chest of an elder who lies on the ground – almost certainly David's father, Jesse. Among the branches are a number of figures, two of which are clearly distinguishable: David, holding a musical instrument, and Solomon, with the royal sceptre in his right hand. Above the tree top and free of the branches is the Virgin Mary. The fact that she is not touching the branches may be a reference to belief in the Compostela church, even as early as the 12th century, in the mystery of the Immaculate Conception – which was not to be defined as a dogma until the 19th century.

The capital displays the Holy Trinity, i.e. the divinity of Christ, through the customary iconography: the Father is a crowned elder with the Son upon his knee. The Holy Spirit is symbolized by a dove, recalling the passage in the gospel on the baptism of Christ, in which it is written, "And Jesus, when he was baptised, went up straightway out of the water: and lo, the heavens were opened unto him, and he saw the Spirit of God descending like a dove and lighting upon him." The dove and fire are images used in the Holy Scriptures to symbolize the Holy Spirit, undoubtedly to emphasise the fire of the love which the Holy Spirit kindles in the hearts of men and the purity instilled by his gifts.

"Santo dos Croques"

Traditionally this Galician name is given to the kneeling figure behind the Pórtico de la Gloria and facing the high altar. It is

(Left) spaces between the branches of the tree in which folk insert their fingers in the belief that they will receive as many mercies as there are fingers on both hands. (Above) Santo dos Croques *on the trumeau of the* Pórtico de la Gloria.

"Santo dos Croques"

At the rear of the Pórtico, behind the trumeau and facing the high altar is an image of a young man in an attitude of prayer. A cartouche in his hand bears the inscription *Architectus*. The figure is believed to represent master Mateo, who in this way not only "signed" his exceptional work but also revealed his deep Christian faith by depicting himself as giving thanks to God through St James for the inspiration he received to carry it out.

Detail from the patriarchs of Jesse: David and Solomon, on the trumeau.

believed to be a self-portrait of master Mateo. The story goes that the Pórtico's master mason had used his own likeness for one of the figures on the inner face and that the Archbishop reproached him for his effrontery in including himself among the representatives of the Church Triumphant when he was no more than a member of the Church Militant. The master then decided to render himself in this humble and thankful attitude. If "croque" is a Galician word, then it means "a blow, either given by or received on the head" and pilgrims usually bring their heads close to that of the statue in the hope of receiving some of Mateo's inspiration. According to other theories, "croque" comes from a word in the language of Occitan, Provençal or Limousin meaning "curl", which would make the figure "the Curly-haired Saint".

(Left) the Virgin Mary on the trumeau of the Pórtico de la Gloria *and (right) the Sacristy doorway.*

In addition to the popular rite of butting master Mateo's head, pilgrims also insert their fingers in the spaces between the branches of the tree in the central column. Although it is said that the pilgrim will thus receive as many mercies as there are fingers on both hands, the church authorities make no claim of this kind.

V THE RADIATING CHAPELS

Towards the Ambulatory

A door on the south side-aisle towards the east end leads to the Relics Chapel and St. Ferdinand's Chapel (now the Treasury, discussed later). The first door on the south transept leads to the

The Sacristy Door
The Sacristy Door is a beautiful Plateresque work made, together with the Cloister door, by the architect Juan de Álava in 1527.

The Clavijo tympanum.

The legend of the Battle of Clavijo
The legend of how the apostle St James appeared to the Asturian king Ramiro I and aided him against the troops of the king of Córdoba, Abd ar-Rahman II, at the Battle of Clavijo, is told in the "Privilegio de los Votos" of 1150. This document also refers to the one hundred maidens paid in tribute each year since the times of the Gothic king Rodrigo (710-711) and Mauregato (783-789) by the kingdom of Asturias to the Muslim king of Córdoba. With this victory Ramiro I abolished payment of the tribute.

Sacristy (not open to the public), which formed part of the work carried out to construct the Relics Chapel in the 16th century and contains 25 paintings on copper: the twelve in the lower section are 18th-century Flemish paintings depicting the 12 articles of the Creed, each attributed to an apostle, while the remaining 13 depict scenes from the life of Christ and the Virgin Mary. The Sacristy also contains canvases by Gregorio Ferro, Juan Antonio Bouzas and Modesto Brocos. The next door leads to the cloisters and museums. Beside it, the **Clavijo Tympanum** depicts maidens giving thanks to St. James for saving them from forfeiture to the Muslims in payment of tribute. The sculptures came from the cloisters, which were built on the orders of Archbishop Gelmírez. The stoup in the opposite corner is believed to have come from the 9th-century church and is said to have been used by Almanzor to water his horse.

The construction of the **Our Lady of the Pillar Chapel** was financed by Archbishop Antonio de Monroy in the 17th century. The mausoleum containing his remains is surmounted with an orant statue carved by Fernández de Sande. The chapel displays the work of two Baroque master masons, Andrade and Casas. The dome is octagonal and the marble altarpiece was designed by Casas and built by Romay. The stone image of Our Lady of the Pillar was brought from Saragossa, while the other figures were made by Sande, who used fossilised shells to adorn the Apostle's cape.

Built in the Flamboyant style, the next chapel has two names: **The Pietà**, due to its advocation, and **The Mondragón**, after its founder, Canon Juan Ibáñez de Mondragón, who lived in the 16th century. The Pietà, or Descent from the Cross, is of baked clay, although some say that it is pumice from Vesuvius. The next chapel, which has three names – **St Peter's, La Azucena** and ***El Magistral***

(Left) the Our Lady of the Pillar Chapel and (right) the altarpiece in the Mondragón Chapel.

The Mondragón Chapel

This chapel was named after its founder, Canon Juan Ibáñez de Mondragón, although it is also known by the name of its patron, the Marqués de Santa Cruz de Rivadulla. The site may correspond to that formerly occupied by the old San Pelayo door. It was built in the Flamboyant Gothic style in 1525 by Jácome García.

The Puerta Santa *viewed from inside the cathedral.*

The "Puerta Santa"
The "Holy Door" or "Door of Forgiveness" (although this name is commonly given to the façade which leads up to it) is flanked by two polychrome stone sculptures made in master Mateo's workshop. It is opened on the 31st December of years previous to "Holy Years" and is closed again on the evening of the following 31st December.

(referring to the fact that its patron is the canon who holds this position) – was founded by Mencía de Andrade in 1571. The Baroque altarpiece was designed by Fernando de Casas and built by Francisco das Moas. The image of St Judas Thaddaeus is deeply venerated as the patron of desperate cases.

The Puerta Santa and the Saviour Chapel

The Puerta Santa ("Holy Door") is opened only during a "Holy Year", i.e. when the feast day of the martyrdom of St James the Great (25th July) falls on a Sunday (in a sequence of 11-6-5-6 years). It is one of the seven minor doors mentioned in the *Codex Calixtinus*, the first guide to the Pilgrim Route to Santiago, written in the 12th century by order of Pope Calixtus II. In the cartouches to

either side of the door, a Latin inscription reads, "All the nations shall come and say: Glory to Thee, O Lord."

The **Saviour Chapel** was the first to be built; indeed, the work on the current cathedral began with the construction of this chapel in 1075. Inscriptions on the two capitals at the entrance state that work began in the times of Bishop Diego Peláez and Alfonso VI. A similar inscription was also carved on the walls, but most of it was destroyed when the niches were built. On this site Archbishop Alonso de Fonseca situated the "Compostela Office", which issued certificates to the effect that pilgrims had completed their pilgrimage; the certificate is still issued today, providing the pilgrim has completed the route and brings a signed statement to this effect. Also stationed here were the priests known as

The altarpiece in the Saviour Chapel.

The Saviour Chapel
Work began on the Cathedral in 1075 with the construction of the Saviour or St Louis King of France Chapel, which has retained its original layout and ornamentation. The capitals display the first manifestations of Romanesque art in the Cathedral. It was consecrated by Bishop Gelmírez in 1102.

Our Lady of Walsingham in the Our Lady of the Snows Chapel.

The Our Lady of the Snows or España Chapel was founded in the late-14th or early-15th century by Juan Miguélez de Camiño and completed with funds provided by Fernán González do Preguntoiro. This is confirmed by an inscription on the basket-handle arch at the entrance.

Due to the Romanesque walls of the adjacent chapels, it is shaped like an irregular pentagon. It has a vault of irregular ribs that is supported by columns with capitals adorned with vegetal motifs.

lenguajeros who confessed pilgrims in their own language before they attended Holy Communion and were issued with their official certificates.

The polychrome stone altar was designed by Juan de Álava and financed by Archbishop Alonso III de Fonseca (16th century) and two saintly bishops of Compostela – Rosendo and Pedro de Mezonzo (to whom the *Salve* is attributed). The Fonseca arms, which displays five stars, recalls the archbishop's generosity in providing the ornamentation of this chapel which in all other respects has remained unchanged since its Romanesque construction.

The chapel is also known as both the **French Chapel** – as Charles V the Wise of France established a foundation in 1380 for the celebration of holy mass in the chapel and – when Louis XI endorsed the foundation in the 15th century – the **St. Louis King of France Chapel**.

The chapel opposite (and directly behind the high altar) formerly served as the sacristy, a confessional and the "Compostela Issuing Office" until Alfonso III had these functions transferred to the Saviour Chapel. At that time it was known as both the **Confession Chapel** and the **Mary Magdalene Chapel**, in honour of this most model penitent. There is another image of Mary Magdalene on the altar in the Saviour Chapel. The altarpiece, which was made by Pedro de Valle in 1671, displays three scenes from the life of St. James the Great: his martyrdom; the transference of his remains; and his burial. Between the altar and the altarpiece the star which surmounts the Apostle's mausoleum can be seen. In front of the altar is the spot where in 1589 Archbishop Juan de Sanclemente ordered the Apostle's remains hidden so that they would not be plundered by the Englishman Drake.

(Left) exterior view of the Our Lady of the Snows Chapel and (right) the altarpiece inside.

(Top left) St John's Chapel and (top right) the tomb of Canon Diego de Castilla in St Bartholomew's Chapel. (Bottom) St Bartholomew's Chapel.

From the Our Lady of the Snows Chapel to the Holy Spirit Chapel.

Dedicated to the Virgin Mary, the next chapel is known both as the **Our Lady of the Snows Chapel** and the **España Chapel** after its patrons, the España family, some of whose members (with others from the Torrado and Arousa families) are buried here. The arch at the entrance dates from the 16th century, while the cross, installed at the time of the chapel's consecration, was made in 1211. The ceiling is an irregular ribbed vault. The Neo-Gothic altar was made by Magariños in the 20th century. The image of Our Lady was made by Gregorio Fernández in 1747. The two other images – Our Lady of Walsingham (English) and Our Lady of Montserrat (Catalan) – date from the latter half of this century. The Brotherhood of St Eligius, patron saint of silversmiths, was founded in this chapel.

In the 16th century, Jácome García made alterations to the **Chapel of St John the Apostle** and **St Susanna** (co-patron of the city of Santiago de Compostela). The chapel was named after the images on the Baroque altarpiece of St John (15th century) and St Susanna, carved by Mariñas in 1902, although for centuries it was known as the Parish Church of St John the Apostle. The image of St Dominic of the Way, donated by the Ministry of Public Works in the Holy Year of 1965, was made by Frechilla.

(Top) detail from the tomb of Archbishop Alonso S. Moscoso and (bottom) the tomb of Juan de Melgarejo.

(Right) the image of Our Lady in the Chapel of the Immaculate Conception and (left) view of the chapel.

The Chapel of the Immaculate Conception

The Chapel of the Immaculate Conception, also known as the Chapel of the Prima Brotherhood and the Chapel of Los Clérigos de Coro, dates from 1525. It was built on the site of the old radiating chapel of Santa Cruz by master Jácome García according to the plans of Juan de Álava. The polychrome wood-carving of Our Lady of O and the Child is curious, as the cross held by the Child links Christ's death with his birth.

The name of the original Chapel of Santa Fe de Conques was changed to that of **Our Lady of Good Counsel** and **St Bartholomew.** It was originally dedicated to the Virgin Mary only but when Canon Gómez Rodríguez de Sotomayor established the foundation of St Bartholomew in 1516, Bartholomew's name was added. Particularly interesting are the capitals. The small Plateresque altarpiece was made by the Flemish woodcarver Mateo Arnao, who also carved the Coimbra marble tomb of Peter the Cruel's great-grandson, Canon Diego de Castilla (d. 1521).

There are two entrances to the **Chapel of the Immaculate Conception**. The original one on the left led to the Holy Cross Chapel. In 1525, the Brotherhood of the Prima Clerics (this room is also known as the **Prima Chapel**) was granted permission to enlarge its cathedral headquarters and dedicate an altar to the Immaculate Conception. The arch on the right was built at this time.

The stone image of the Immaculate Conception was carved by Cornelis of Holland in the 16th century and was repainted and bejewelled in the 18th century. Its iconography included a novelty – the Virgin Mary holding the Child in her arms and the Child holding a cross in its hand. The Descent from the Cross was carved by Diego Fernández de Sande in 1721, while all the other figures were made by Antonio Alfonsín and Manuel de Leis. Virtually indistinguishable in the floor is the tomb of the Baroque master mason Domingo Antonio de Andrade.

Since the 13th century the site of one of the Cathedral's original doors, that of St Mary, has been occupied by the **Holy Spirit Chapel**, once the headquarters of the *Sancti Spiritus* Chaplains (subsequently known as the *Sancti Spiritus* Prebendaries). The chapel was enlarged in the 14th century and further alterations became necessary in the 16th and 17th centuries. The

The Holy Spirit Chapel.

The Holy Spirit Chapel
This chapel was founded in the late-13th century by Pedro Vidal, who provided an endowment for matins to be said in it by twelve chaplains. These were known as the *Sancti Spiritus* Chaplains until the middle of the 15th century, when Archbishop Álvaro Núñez de Isorna founded a college for them and appointed them *Racioneros* or Prebendaries.

The Church of La Corticela.

The Parish Church of La Corticela
This is known to be one of the oldest churches in Santiago, for as early as the 9th century it was an oratory which depended on the nearby Benedictine monastery. When the Benedictine order built the Church of San Martín and its oratory the monks continued to attend La Corticela in order to retain entitlement to certain rights connected with it. Since the earliest times it has been a parish church for foreigners and was once staffed by priests known as *lenguajeros* who confessed pilgrims in their own languages.

altar and the image of Our Lady of Solitude, originally in the retrochoir, were transferred to the chapel in 1945. The image of the Virgin Mary was made in Madrid in 1666. The embroidered mantle was donated by Archbishop Rafael de Vélez in the 19th century. The silver altar and steps were made in the 18th century by Antonio Morales and the pedestal, the angels and the ornaments were made by Francisco Rodríguez. The Calvary dates from the 15th century.

A Parish Church for Foreign and Basque Pilgrims

At this point a staircase leads up to the Parish Church of **La Corticela**, once an oratory in which the Benedictine monks venerated the Apostle. Although the current building is the result of work carried out between the 11th and early-13th century, it was restored in the middle of this century. It was founded in the Middle Ages as a parish church for foreign and Basque pilgrims.

(Left) St Catherine's Chapel and (right) the Communion Chapel.

Romanesque like all the church, the frontispiece displays an Adoration of the Magi, a very common motif in Compostela as the three kings who came to adore Christ were pilgrims as well as representatives of different peoples, all of which underlines the universal nature of pilgrimage to Santiago de Compostela. Our Lady of Consolation presides over the church. The Christ Child of Prague was the patron of the Tecelanes. Furthermore, the jetworkers' guild once had an image of their patron, St Stephen, here. The cults of the "Prayer of Jesus in the Garden" and "Our Lady of the Miraculous Medal" are also extremely popular in this church although their iconography does not match the architectural purity of this building which was not originally connected to the Cathedral.

To the right, the chapel dedicated to **St Andrew** was the seat of the parish of the same name previously situated in the area now occupied by the Our Lady of the Pillar Chapel. The side altars are dedicated to Our Lady of Mount Carmel and to St Joseph. In a

St Catherine's Chapel

Situated on the west side of the north transept, until the beginning of this century St Catherine's chapel was a royal pantheon. The tombs were subsequently transferred to the Relics Chapel, which suggests that it was built long before the 16th century. Another possible construction date is 13th March 1544, when an endowment was made to it by Canon Lope Sánchez de Ulloa, whose arms are displayed on the screen.

St James the Knight or Moorslayer, carved by Gambino in the 18th century.

The Christ of Burgos.

niche, an image of Our Lady of Luján, donated by the Doello-Teruelos, replaced an earlier one brought to the church by Eva Perón. The chapel was built in the 17th century.

VI THE CHAPELS ON THE NORTH SIDE-AISLE

From St Anthony's Chapel to the Christ of Burgos Chapel

St Anthony's Chapel, which took over the functions of St Nicholas's Chapel when it was demolished to make way for the Church of La Corticela, was once also the parish see of St Fructuosus (now in the old Church of Las Angustias de Abajo). The altarpiece dates from the 18th century. The image of Our Lady of Fátima was brought to the chapel from the Portuguese village in 1948.

The next chapel after the Azabachería entrance is **St Catherine's Chapel**, dedicated to the saint of Alexandria and built before the 16th century. This chapel contains a reproduction of the apparitions of the Virgin Mary in Lourdes.

The image of **St James the Knight** was made by Gambino in the latter half of the 18th century. This depiction of St James represents the Apostle's protection of the Spanish nation over the centuries and is based on the tradition of his appearance to Ramiro I at the Battle of Clavijo (actually fought by Ordoño I). It is displayed on a door which once led to the next chapel, that of **Lope de Mendoza**, named after its founder, who was Archbishop of Santiago de Compostela from 1399 to 1445, and which is also known as the **Communion Chapel** and the **Sacred Heart Chapel**. To the right of the entrance, the Archbishop kneels at the feet of the alabaster image of Our Lady of Forgiveness begging for God's mercy through her intercession. The present chapel, a Neo-Classical rotunda with a dome, was built in the 18th century on the orders of Archbishop Rajoy; it was designed by Ferro Caaveiro and constructed by Del Río and Nogueira. Made by Lens, the altarpiece was originally situated in the Relics Chapel. The statues of four doctors of the Church in niches were carved by Gregorio Español and Juan Vila. In the 16th and 17th centuries university degrees were awarded here. Archbishops Mendoza and Rajoy are buried in this chapel.

The construction of the **Christ of Burgos** or **Carrillo Chapel** was ordered by another archbishop, Pedro Carrillo y Acuña. Built in 1665 by Melchor de Velasco y Agüero, it stands on a Greek cross plan and has a coffered dome. A copy of the original, the fine image of Christ was carved in Burgos in 1754. The Baroque side altars, made by Melchor de Prado, display two scenes from the gospel:

(Left) a bust of St James the Less, son of Alphaeus, and (right) an image of St James the Pilgrim.

the intercession of St Salome on behalf of her children, on the right; and St Peter weeping after his denial of Christ, on the left. The tombs at the sides are of Archbishops Carrillo and García Cuesta, while the one in the floor is of Zacarías Martínez Núñez, another Archbishop of Santiago.

THE MUSEUMS

With the visit to the interior of the Cathedral concluded, the next rooms are the Museums, two of which are inside the Cathedral and one (discussed later) outside it.

I THE RELICS CHAPEL AND THE TREASURY

The Relics Chapel, which is also known as St Ferdinand's Chapel, contains some of the Cathedral's greatest treasures and stands opposite the Chapel of the Christ of Burgos on the other side of the Cathedral.

Normally the **Relics Chapel** is open to the public for only half an hour each day, during the celebration of mass (9.30 a.m. on working days). Designed by Juan de Álava, the chapel was built between 1521 and 1529. In 1921 Fernando Cabrera's altarpiece

The Relics Chapel
Particularly important among the items in the Relics Chapel are: a bust of St James, son of Alphaeus, carved in the 16th century and mounted with precious stones, cameos and a delicately worked diadem; and a silver-gilt image of St James the Pilgrim sent to Santiago from Paris by Jean de Roucel and his wife in the 15th century.

Image of St Teresa.

and with it almost all the images made by Gregorio Español were destroyed by fire. In 1925 Maximino Magariños made a new cedarwood altarpiece to a design by Rafael de la Torre. Most of the chapel can be seen from the glass door at the entrance.

The one hundred and forty relics venerated in this area are contained in urns, busts, glass cases and images. Particularly important is the head of St James the Less. It is contained in a silver bust with an enamelled face – donated by Archbishop Berenguel de Landoira in the 14th century – and bedecked with a necklace donated by Suero de Quiñones in the 15th century. Also important is a 13th-14th century image of St James the Great donated by the Parisian Coquatriz and containing a bone. Finally, a 19th-century image of St Teresa of Jesus contains one of the saint of Avila's teeth and her signature.

Among the many other objects displayed in this chapel are: a reproduction of a cross donated by Alfonso III in 874; a 16th-century Italian rock crystal and gold pax donated by Charles II in 1638; silver cornucopias adorned with precious stones and biblical motifs; a small alabaster altarpiece donated by the English priest Gudgar in 1456; a chalice and paten said to have belonged to St Rudesind; and a silver-gilt St James the Pilgrim sent to the Cathedral from Paris in the 15th century.

From outside the chapel it is not possible to see the royal tombs, which were transferred here from St Catherine's Chapel in 1535. The tombs on the right contain the remains of Ferdinand II of León (whose recumbent statue may have been made by Mateo), Alfonso IX, Conde Traba and Don Pedro Froilaz; on the left are the tombs of Doña Berenguela, wife of Alfonso VII, Conde Ramón de Borgoña, Alfonso's father, and Juana de Castro, wife of king Peter I of Castile.

The monstrance in St Ferdinand's Chapel.

The vestibule contains various paintings by Cancela dating from the 19th century, one depicting the appearance of the Virgin Mary to St Felix of Catalicio and attributed to Murillo, as well as the tomb stone of Bishop Theodomir, who died in 847. It was during Theodomir's pontificate when the remains of St James the Great were rediscovered, prompting the bishop's wish to be buried close to the Apostle's tomb rather than in the capital of his see, Iria Flavia (situated between Compostela and Padrón).

For a period of almost a hundred years during the 16th and 17th centuries **St. Ferdinand's Chapel** served as the Relics Chapel. It was named after Ferdinand III the saint, who called himself "the standard bearer of St. James". Ferdinand accompanied his father, Alfonso IX, at the consecration of the cathedral in 1211, and, as king in 1232, returned to Compostela as a pilgrim. His image, on

(Left) a bust of St Paulina and (right) a detail from the tomb of St Ferdinand II of León.

the altar, was carved by Seoane in 1676. The frescoes of the Ascension of Christ and the Assumption of the Virgin were painted in 1540.

The silver-gilt monstrance was made by Antonio de Arfe in the 16th century. Below it are six reliefs with scenes from the life of St James, beginning with his calling by Jesus and ending with the transference of his remains; one other scene depicts the miracle of the hanged man and the resuscitated cockerel as told in the *Codex Calixtinus.* Twenty-four smaller reliefs depict scenes from the life of Christ. Homage is also paid to the Eucharist through four figures of doctors of the Church. The coral image of St. Christopher on a silver and bronze background is Italian and is said to have been donated to the Cathedral by John of Austria. The jet image of St James was made by E. Mayer in 1919. The silver cup, which is used in the "Ofrenda Nacional" or "National Offering" ceremony, was donated by the Duke of Montpensier and his wife, Isabella II's sister. The hammer is one of those used to open the Puerta Santa. The chapel also contains: shell-shaped trays (the scallop-shell is traditionally associated with St James); various chalices, paxes and other liturgical objects; a pair of rock crystal candelabra; a crucifix with gold mountings, also of rock crystal (the figure of Christ is also of gold); a display cabinet with the hat of Cardinal Quiroga Palacios, who died in 1971; and a triptych donated to the cardinal by the authorities of his province of origin, Orense. The last monstrance is adorned with jewels donated by the Ferreiro de la Maza family. Both it and the triptych from Orense were made in the workshop of Ángel Iglesias. Among the ornaments are 16th-century copes and 18th-century chasubles and dalmatics.

The Relics Chapel (continued)
The chapel also contains the head of St Paulina, brought from Cologne by Archbishop Gaspar de Ábalos in 1544.
The silver bust with an enamelled face was made by Jorge Cerdeira in 1533.
Also in the chapel are a number of royal tombs transferred from St Catherine's Chapel in 1536.
In the photograph, the tomb (in all likelihood by master Mateo) of Ferdinand II of León, who died in 1118.

View of the Cloisters.

The Cloisters
This area is a fine example of the Castilian Gothic style with Renaissance influence. The cresting is extremely beautiful. The fascia with "Roman" ornamentation curves to accommodate the coats of arms of the great patrons of this work – Archbishops Fonseca, Taaber and Sanclemente. At the centre of the courtyard is a large stone basin from the Azabachería façade; it originally belonged to the fountain at the "Paradise" door mentioned in the *Codex Calixtinus.* The three sun dials above the arches date from 1601.

II THE CLOISTERS

The second door on the south transept leads to the **Cloisters** and **Museums**. These are the Cathedral's third cloisters, the first having been built in the 12th century, possibly by master Mateo, when Gelmírez was archbishop, and the second in the 13th century. Among the artists and craftsmen who worked on the current cloisters (1521-1590) were Juan de Álava, Jácome García, Rodrigo Gil de Hontañón, Juan de Herrera and Gaspar de Arce. The initiative for the project came from Archbishop Alonso III of Fonseca, as is corroborated by his arms at the end of the corridor.

III THE DAWN CHAPEL AND THE ARCHIVES

The **Dawn Chapel** stands at the end of the north cloister close to the Museum. It was founded in 1529 by Canon Gómez

Vallo so that mass could be celebrated there each day at daybreak, hence the chapel's name. The 18th-century altarpiece, which replaced one made previously by Cornelis of Holland, displays a depiction of the Transfiguration.

On the southwest corner of the cloisters are the **Chapter Archives**, which contain extremely important documents relevant not only to the Cathedral but also to the whole of Galicia; some, such as those referring to the "Voto de Santiago" ("Santiago Offering"), are relevant to an even greater geographical area. Particularly valuable are the *Codex Calixtinus*, Registers A, B, C and D, which contain records dating from the 9th to the 14th century, and original diplomas, etc. The Archives are open to researchers.

The Dawn Chapel.

IV THE LIBRARY AND THE CHAPTER HOUSE

On the west side of the cloisters are two rooms. The first is the **Chapter Library**, whose collections are due to the generosity of Canons Pedro de Acuña Malvar and Diego Juan de Ulloa. It was built by Ferro Caaveiro and Arias Varela in the 18th century. The movable pulpit dates from the same period. The room is adorned with frescoes and also with sanguines.

The Archives.

View of the gallery around the Tapestry Museum.

The Chapter Library
This library is full of curious books, including a number of incunabula. It was built in the 18th century. Particularly interesting are the frescoes and sanguines on the ceiling and the frieze depicting the life, martyrdom and miracles of St James the Great. At the corners are portraits of Doctors of the Church. The themes depicted in the medallions above the doors and the paintings on the west wall are Abraham's sacrifice of Isaac, the Queen of Sheba's visit to Solomon and the flagellation of St Roch.

To the left are two ***botafumeiros***. The first was donated by the "Brotherhood of Provisional Standard-bearers" in 1971, while the second was made in 1851. The *botafumeiro* is known to have existed as early as the 14th century and must originally have been used to add more solemnity to religious occasions and also to freshen the air in the Cathedral at those times of the year when it was filled day and night with travel-stained pilgrims. It weighs 54 kilos.

The *botafumeiro* is used before mass, when the archbishop leads a procession, on high feast days and for certain pilgrimages to the Cathedral. During processions it is used to cense the presiding relic. Eight men known as *tiraboleiros* (a Galician form of the Latin *thuribularii*) pull on ropes to make the burner swing, almost to the ceiling, in a 50-metre arc in the direction of the arms of the transept. The burner is said to have broken free on various occasions, although never with casualties. One such occasion was in 1501, in the presence of the Infanta Catalina, who was on her way

Pictures of the silver botafumeiro *and the* tiraboleiros. *The* botafumeiro *was made in 1851 by Losada to replace the one taken by the French in 1809.*

The Chapter House. Facing page, the Library

to England to marry Arthur, Prince of Wales; another was in 1662. On other occasions a few scratches and bruises have been received by onlookers who came too close.

The next room is the **Chapter House**, so named because it is the official meeting place of the cathedral canons, who form the "Chapter" (from the Latin "Capitulum" meaning "a meeting of canons"). Although the architectural aspects of this room may reflect the influence of Casas y Nóvoa, it was actually designed by Luca Ferro Caaveiro. The granite vault was stuccoed and gilded by Aguiar. The frontal was made by Bartolomé Sernini, who worked on the Royal Palace of Madrid; the St James the Pilgrim is by Gambino; the canopy, made at the Royal Tapestry Factory of Madrid, was designed by Guillermo de Anglois for Charles III's bed-chamber. Also made at the Royal Factory, the other tapestries (some of which are Flemish) were woven from cartoons by Teniers and depict scenes from the lives of Achilles and Scipio. Also of interest are the 18th-century brazier with motifs alluding to St James and two cases made of lignum vitae inlaid with mother-of-pearl and ivory. The painting

The Chapter House and Library
The old Chapter House and Library were destroyed in a fire in 1751. The new buildings were raised by the architect Luca Ferro Caaveiro, a pupil and successor of the master builder Casas y Nóvoa.

te De us
Deus tu
us oleo leti
tie. lelu
ia
Specie tu

A tapestry from the Santa Bárbara Royal Factory, from a cartoon by Goya.

of Our Lady of Guadalupe was donated by Archbishop Antonio de Monroy, who was born in Mexico.

V THE CATHEDRAL MUSEUMS

The Cathedral Museums consist of three main areas, each with a ticket office. They are the Treasury, the Crypt beneath the Pórtico de la Gloria, and the Archaeological and Tapestry Museums (access via the Plaza de España entrance to the right of the Obradoiro façade). In the following brief descriptions of their contents, the Archaeological and Tapestry Museums will be discussed first.

(Facing page) tapestries depicting scenes from the life of Achilles, from cartoons by Rubens.

Ground floor

This floor consists of four rooms, the last of which displays new exhibits recovered from part of the work of master Mateo.

The first room exhibits items unearthed in excavations carried out over various centuries. They date from the 1st to the 10th century and illustrate circumstances surrounding the Apostle's tomb. Also exhibited are items from the two churches – raised by Alfonso II and Alfonso III in the 9th century – which existed before the present Cathedral was built. Furthermore, on pieces such as the Setecoros and Carcacía capitals (which come from sites close to the first diocesan see, Iria Flavia) there are illustrations of early Christianity in this region of Galicia.

The second room is dedicated to the current Cathedral, built on the orders of Alfonso VI. The items are divided into two groups according to their dates. The first group covers the time of Bernardo the Elder (1075-1088) and includes moulds from the original capitals, while the second (1100-1165) covers the time of master Esteban and his work on the Platerías façade (the only work by this builder and his school to have survived), and consists of marble

The 14th-century tympanum with the Adoration of the Magi.

Our Lady of Expectation *or* of O.

shafts and depictions of Adam and Eve, the month of February, and Christ in Majesty.

The third room covers the period (1165-1211) when master Mateo and his assistants completed their work. In 1211 the Cathedral was consecrated for the last time. The items corresponding to this period include an arch, rose windows, imposts with angels, sculptures and capitals. Also exhibited is a 17th-century drawing of the west end by Canon Vega y Verdugo.

The fourth room displays the remains of the mediaeval road known as the "Rúa de Valladares", milestones, alms boxes, Roman tombstones and remains from the 13th-century mediaeval cloisters. Especially important are a number of items from master Mateo's choir and the plans for this great work.

The mezzanine

The first room displays items dating from the 13th to 16th century, the most important being: an anonymous 15th-century wood and alabaster altarpiece dedicated to St James and named after its donor, the English priest Gudgar; a tympanum depicting the entrance of Jesus into Jerusalem; a 13th-century seated image of St James; a 14th-century tympanum depicting the Adoration of the Magi; a 16th-century Christ Crucified by Celma; Our Lady of Expectation (also known as Our Lady of O); the Archangel Gabriel, from the 15th century; and The Three

The body of St James on Queen Lupa's oxcart; polychrome wood, in the Archaeological Museum.

St Michael the Archangel weighing souls.

Generations (Anne, Mary and the Child), which are in the Hispanic-Flemish style.

The second room contains sculptures dating from the 13th to 19th century, particularly important being reliefs by Gregorio Español of the life of St James (from the altarpiece in the Relics Chapel before it was destroyed by fire).

The third room has recently been dedicated to numismatics and important documents related to St James. The items include a major collection of coins made at the Santiago de Compostela mint, other coins found during excavations and coins brought from different countries by pilgrims in the Holy Year of 1976.

Upper floor

The first room contains tapestries by Teniers, Ginés de Aguirre and Castillo. The largest, depicting the Holy Family asking hunters for food, is by Castillo. All were made at the Royal Tapestry Factory in Madrid. There are also two items of Cordovan leather. The pennant (17.5 metres in length) from the flagship at the Battle of Lepanto was donated by John of Austria in 1571.

The second room contains tapestries depicting scenes from the story of Achilles and other mythological themes. The cartoons were made by Rubens and Van Thulden at the workshops of Jan Raëz and Erasmus Oorlofs in Brussels. The chest for holding ornaments dates from the 18th century.

Registers.

The third room contains tapestries (at the top) with scenes of rural life made at the Royal Tapestry Factory in Madrid from cartoons by Teniers. The *Game of Skittles,* however, apparently came from Melter's workshop in Lille, and the beggar may have been painted by Antonio González Ruiz. In addition to the tapestries there are paxes and images, including a polychrome terracotta Our Lady Nursing the Child made by the sculptress Roldán (better known as "La Roldana") and a jet St James by Mayer.

The fourth room contains tapestries from cartoons by Bayeu and González Ruiz. The pig-slaughtering scene dates from Teniers's blue period and was made at Melter's workshop in Lille.

The fifth room exhibits tapestries made from cartoons by Goya and donated by Charles IV to his Foreign Secretary, Pedro de Acuña, canon of the Cathedral. All were made at the Santa Bárbara Royal Tapestry Factory. The pictures were painted in the 17th century by Gregorio Ferro, the Compostela artist who was appointed Director of the Royal Academy of San Fernando in preference to Goya.

On leaving this room, the visitor may view the Cloisters (page 54), where the Archives (open only to researchers) and the Dawn Chapel are situated.

A visit to the Library and Chapter House (pages 55-60) is recommended before proceeding to the Treasury (pages 51-53).

VI THE ARCHAEOLOGICAL MUSEUM

The two rooms which form the Archaeological Museum are situated below the Tapestry Museum.

At the entrance to the lower room, a cast of St James between cypresses is based on master Esteban's work on the Platerías façade (1100). Also important is the rose window (replaced by the current Baroque one) from the Pórtico de la Gloria and made, as were several items from the choir stalls, at Mateo's workshop. Finally, also displayed are a number of objects unearthed during excavations carried out under the Cathedral after 1946. Leaving this room, another area to the right contains road paving, a picture of master Mateo's Choir and various pieces from it, and the Caligula milestone, which dates from 40 A.D.

VII THE CRYPT BENEATH THE PÓRTICO

One possibility before entering the Cathedral to view the items displayed in the Treasury is to visit what is wrongly known as the Old Cathedral. Lying beneath the main staircase, at the same level as

View of the Crypt in the Old Cathedral.

the square, this area is, in fact, no more than a crypt made by master Mateo to compensate for the unevenness of the ground and so be able to build this three-floor construction. The lowest level is the Crypt, dedicated to the veneration of the apostle St James the Less, son of Alphaeus, which Mateo was able to complete before his death. The bosses of the ribbed vaults display an angel with laws, by Mateo, and the moon, by master Ropas Mojadas, who also made a number of pieces on the Crypt's old frontispiece.

Also admirable are the copies of the musical instruments held by the elders on the Pórtico de la Gloria; they were studied by Professor López Calo and financed by the *Fundación Barrié de la Maza.*

The Crypt or Old Cathedral

Believed by many to have been built by Archbishop Gelmírez, the Crypt appears to date from the late-11th century. Another theory holds that it was built by master Mateo around 1168. However, Romanesque elements in the early-Gothic structure have prompted the theory that Mateo did not actually build the Crypt but only made alterations to it.

This book, published by Aldeasa, was printed
in Madrid on 19th May 1998 at
Estudios Gráficos Europeos